The Pirate and the Potter Family

Sick As a Parrot

Chapter | Page

Written by Michaela Morgan
Illustrated by Martin Chatterton

Chapter 1
The Potters Get a Shock

and Mum was tidying the baby.

The dog was already tidy.

Soon, there was nothing left to tidy.

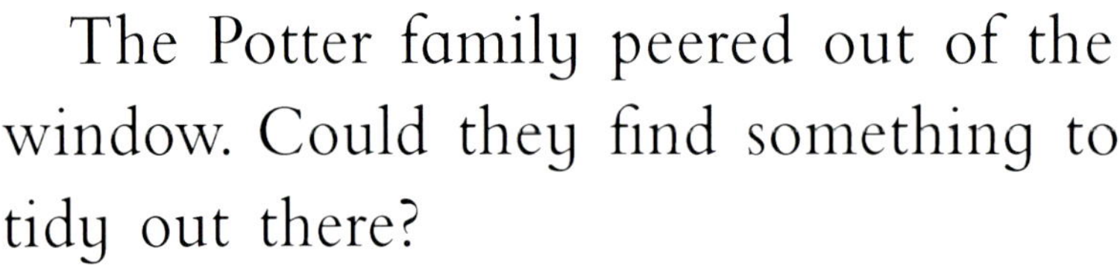

The Potter family peered out of the window. Could they find something to tidy out there?

"What's that?" gasped Dad. There, lying in the garden, was an enormous, messy heap. What was it?

seaweed?

The Potters went out to look.

It was a pirate! He was a mess. He was dressed in smelly old rags and he did not look tidy at all. He had a parrot on his arm. It had lost a lot of its feathers. It was shabby. It was gloomy. It was a very sick parrot.

"What are you doing in our garden?" Mum demanded. Then, to everyone's surprise, the big, grubby pirate started crying. He blubbed and he sobbed. Huge tears ran down his face.

"There, there, dear," said Gran. "Here's a hanky. Have a good blow and tell us all about it."

Chapter 2
Meet Captain Kev

"My name be Cap'n Kevin Kerfuffle," he said. "I be a good, friendly pirate. I sail the seven seas with my parrot. But my feathered friend is sick ..."

"Sick!" the parrot repeated.

"So I came ashore to find a vet ..."

"Find a vet!" the parrot begged.

The Potters didn't know what to do with this shabby, smelly pirate.

"I have a plan!" said Gran. "Leave your parrot with us. We can look after it and you can go back to sea."

"Thank ye kindly," Captain Kev smiled, "but I couldn't leave 'im behind. I've loved 'im since he were an egg."

That is how the Potter family came to have a pirate – and a parrot – living in their attic.
The pirate helped the Potter family.

He even changed the baby's nappy.

What shall we do with the dirty nappy?
What shall we do with the dirty nappy?
What shall we do with the dirty nappy?
Early in the morning.

Peel it off and stuff it in a *bucket*,
Peel it off and stuff it in a *bucket*,
Peel it off and stuff it in a *bucket*,
Early in the morning.

Clean 'im up and dry him nicely,
Clean 'im up and dry him nicely,
Clean 'im up and dry him nicely,
Early in the morning.

Day by day, the pirate was becoming more clean and tidy. Day by day, the Potters were becoming more like pirates. But day by day, even with Gran's care, the parrot stayed the same. This was one sick parrot.

Lilly knew all about parrots now. She had read a book.

They tried everything.
medicine
tickling
keep fit
Nothing worked.

Chapter 3
What a Mess!

My spare leg!
My winter vest!
BUS
BUS
Pet Hints for Pirates
ld bus tickets ... and a very interesting book!

Chapter 4
How to Perk Up Your Parrot

Is your parrot down-at-beak?
Then try this instant parrot perk-up.

Pet Hints for Pirates

"I think we should try this," said Gran.

Soon the Potters were holding a bowl full of tasty bits in front of the parrot.

"Bananas!" muttered the parrot.

"**BATS!**" he shouted.

Bit by bit, the poorly parrot perked up. Then he began to fizz and pop. He gave a very large pop and fell beak-first into the parrot perk-up.
pop!
FIZZ!
He lay there blinking and drinking. Then …

"Chocks away!" squealed the parrot. He whizzed around the room, hiccupping and burping and making little popping noises. He even started to tap dance! He was a truly perked-up parrot.
Hic!

"There!" said Gran. "I reckon your parrot's cured!"

"Parrot's cured!" squawked the parrot. He perched on Gran's head. "Who's a pretty girl, then?" he teased.

Gran blushed. "Who'd like a bit of cake?" she asked.

"Oo-ar, I do be wanting a bit," said Captain Kev. "I do be ..."

"Do-be-dooo!" sang the happy parrot.

Chapter 5
Setting Sail

Captain Kev sniffed the air. "I do be wantin' the smell of salt spray again. Time for me to set sail."

"But we'll miss you!" cried the Potters.

"Well, you lot could come too," said Captain Kev, "but yer far too sensible to sail the seven seas, aren't you?"

The Potters looked thoughtful. Then …
Shiver me timbers!
Ahoy, matey!
Arrr!

They decided to set sail!

“All aboard then,” said Captain Kev.

“All aboard!” echoed the parrot. With one happy burp, he flapped his wings, took flight and off they went.